SHADOWS OF HISTORY:

Unraveling the Great Conspiracy Theories of Our Time

by SEA62 Books Aho

Table Of Contents

Chapter 1: The Origins of
Conspiracy Theories   4

Chapter 2: Government
Cover-Ups Throughout
Time   18

Chapter 3: Celebrities and
Their Secrets   32

Chapter 4: Alien
Encounters and UFO
Sightings   45

Chapter 5: The Dark
World of Secret Societies   57

Chapter 6: Medical and
Pharmaceutical
Conspiracies   71

Chapter 7: Financial and Economic Conspiracies   83

Chapter 8: Technology and Surveillance Conspiracies   95

Chapter 9: Political Conspiracy Theories   108

Chapter 10: Environmental Conspiracy Theories   120

Chapter 11: The Future of Conspiracy Theories   133

Chapter 1: The Origins of Conspiracy Theories

The Birth of Doubt in History

Doubt emerged as a powerful force in history, igniting a transformative movement that challenged the established narratives of societies around the globe. From the ancient skepticism of philosophers questioning the divine right of kings to the modern age's relentless inquiry into governmental actions, the seeds of doubt have always been sown in fertile ground. The curiosity of individuals to seek the truth behind the curtain of authority has led to the birth of various conspiracy theories, shaping our understanding of reality and the structures that govern us. This insatiable quest for knowledge often reveals the fragility of accepted histories, as the shadows cast by doubt give birth to new narratives that demand attention.

As we explore the tapestry of doubt woven throughout history, we find that it has been a constant companion to those in power. Governments and institutions, often shrouded in secrecy, have repeatedly faced scrutiny from those who refuse to accept the status quo. The Watergate scandal stands as a prime example, where journalists, driven by doubt, uncovered a web of deception that shook the very foundations of trust in political institutions. Such revelations serve as a reminder that doubt is not merely an abstract concept; it is a catalyst for change, prompting society to question what it has been told and to seek out the hidden truths that lie beneath.

The rise of technology has further fueled the flames of doubt, particularly in an age where information is at our fingertips. The internet has become a double-edged sword, enabling the rapid dissemination of both facts and misinformation. Conspiracy theories surrounding financial institutions or pharmaceutical companies have gained traction as individuals turn to online platforms to share their suspicions. The ease with which information spreads has led to a renaissance of skepticism, as people now challenge the narratives put forth by those in power. This technological evolution has given birth to a new breed of investigator, one who seeks to peel back the layers of truth in a world filled with conflicting accounts.

In the realm of celebrity culture, doubt manifests in astonishing ways, often leading to wild speculations about the lives of the rich and famous. From whispers of secret societies to the notion that public figures are mere puppets in a grand performance, the allure of the conspiracy theory captivates the public's imagination. Figures like Princess Diana and Michael Jackson have become central to narratives that explore the darker sides of fame and fortune, where doubt transforms tragedy into intrigue. These stories not only entertain but also reflect societal anxieties about trust, privilege, and the unseen forces that shape our lives.

Ultimately, the birth of doubt in history is not merely a phenomenon of the past; it is an enduring aspect of human nature. As we navigate a world rife with contradictions and hidden agendas, the act of questioning becomes essential. Whether in the political arena, the corridors of power, or the glamorous facades of celebrity, doubt invites us to dig deeper, to challenge the narratives that we have been fed, and to uncover the truths that lie beneath. In this thrilling journey through the shadows of history, we discover that doubt is not our enemy; it is our greatest ally in the pursuit of understanding.

The Role of Misinformation

The role of misinformation in the tapestry of conspiracy theories is both fascinating and complex. Throughout history, misinformation has acted as a catalyst, igniting public curiosity and skepticism towards established narratives. The allure of conspiracy theories often lies in their ability to provide alternative explanations for events that seem too convoluted or incomprehensible. This desire for clarity in a chaotic world drives individuals to seek out information that aligns with their beliefs, sometimes disregarding factual accuracy in favor of sensationalism. The seductive nature of these narratives can create a sense of belonging among believers, forging communities united by their shared doubts about official accounts.

Shadows of History: Unraveling the Great Conspiracy Theories of Our Time

In the realm of historical conspiracy theories, misinformation can distort our understanding of pivotal events. Take, for instance, the theories surrounding the assassination of prominent figures like John F. Kennedy or Martin Luther King Jr. Each theory, laden with half-truths and conjecture, often overshadows the documented facts, creating an alternate reality that captivates the imagination. The proliferation of these narratives is fueled by a desire to uncover hidden truths, but they can also lead to a misinformed public, questioning the integrity of historical records and institutions. As a result, the very fabric of history can become tangled in a web of deception, making it imperative to scrutinize the sources that shape our perceptions.

Government cover-ups represent another arena where misinformation thrives. From the Watergate scandal to contemporary surveillance debates, the idea that governments manipulate information to control narratives is deeply ingrained in public consciousness. Theories suggesting that certain events are orchestrated to serve political ends often gain traction because they resonate with a fundamental distrust of authority. This distrust is not unfounded, as real instances of governmental deceit have occurred throughout history. However, the line between justified skepticism and unfounded conspiracy is often blurred, leading to an environment where misinformation can flourish unchecked.

Celebrity conspiracy theories also highlight the role of misinformation in shaping public perception. The fascination with the lives of public figures can lead to wild speculation and exaggerated claims, often propagated through social media and sensationalist news outlets. Whether it's theories about the true nature of a celebrity's death or the supposed hidden connections among Hollywood elites, misinformation can morph into a modern-day folklore, compelling audiences to invest emotionally in narratives that are often devoid of factual basis. This phenomenon underscores how easily misinformation can spread, as the desire to believe in a scandalous secret outweighs the need for verification.

As we navigate the landscape of conspiracy theories, understanding the role of misinformation is crucial for fostering critical thinking. The intersection of technology and misinformation has made it easier than ever to disseminate falsehoods, especially in an age where information is abundant but often unverified. The challenge lies in discerning credible sources from those that perpetuate myths. By developing a skeptical mindset and prioritizing fact-checking, individuals can arm themselves against the tidal wave of misinformation that seeks to obscure the truth. Ultimately, recognizing the potent influence of misinformation not only aids in deciphering conspiracy theories but also empowers individuals to reclaim their agency in a world rife with uncertainty.

The Psychology Behind Belief

The psychology behind belief plays a crucial role in
understanding why conspiracy theories captivate the minds of
so many individuals. At the core of this phenomenon lies a
universal human desire for certainty and control in a chaotic
world. When faced with complex societal issues, individuals
often seek out simple explanations. Conspiracy theories offer a
narrative that brings clarity, attributing significant events to
shadowy figures or secret organizations. This need for clarity
can lead people to embrace these theories, as they provide a
semblance of understanding in an unpredictable environment,
making it easier to digest the complexities of life.

Another key psychological factor is the allure of belonging. Many conspiracy theories thrive within tight-knit communities that share the same beliefs. This communal aspect fosters a sense of identity and purpose, as individuals find camaraderie with like-minded believers. The reinforcement of these beliefs within these groups can create an echo chamber, amplifying their convictions and further entrenching their adherence to the theory. The feeling of being part of an exclusive group that possesses "secret knowledge" is intoxicating, allowing individuals to feel empowered against the perceived ignorance of the mainstream.

Cognitive biases also significantly contribute to the persistence of conspiracy beliefs. The confirmation bias, in particular, leads individuals to seek out information that supports their preexisting beliefs while dismissing contradictory evidence. This behavior can create a self-reinforcing cycle, where believers become increasingly convinced of their theories despite the lack of credible evidence. Furthermore, the proportionality bias—a tendency to believe that big events must have equally significant explanations—fuels the belief in conspiracies. People often struggle to accept that some events are random or the result of mismanagement rather than a grand conspiracy, which makes these theories even more appealing.

Emotional factors cannot be overlooked either. Fear and anxiety about the unknown often drive individuals toward conspiracy theories as a coping mechanism. In times of crisis—be it political turmoil, health emergencies, or environmental disasters—the human psyche seeks comfort in narratives that provide a scapegoat or a clear adversary. Conspiracy theories can serve as an emotional outlet, allowing individuals to channel their frustrations and fears into a narrative that feels more manageable. This emotional investment can make it exceedingly challenging for believers to let go of these theories, even when confronted with contradicting evidence.

Finally, the digital age has transformed the landscape of belief, providing unprecedented access to information and a platform for conspiracy theories to flourish. Social media algorithms often prioritize sensational content, allowing conspiracy theories to spread virally and reach vast audiences. This environment not only reinforces existing beliefs but also attracts new followers, creating a culture where conspiracy theories can thrive with little scrutiny. Understanding the psychology behind belief in conspiracy theories is essential for unraveling their appeal, revealing the intricate interplay of human emotions, cognitive biases, and social dynamics that drive individuals to embrace these captivating narratives.

Chapter 2: Government Cover-Ups Throughout Time

The Watergate Scandal

The Watergate Scandal stands as one of the most significant political conspiracies in American history, captivating the minds of citizens and scholars alike. This scandal not only exposed the underbelly of political machinations but also ignited a fervor for transparency and accountability in government. At its core, the Watergate affair involved a break-in at the Democratic National Committee headquarters in 1972, but its ramifications reached far beyond a mere burglary. It unveiled a labyrinth of deceit, cover-ups, and abuse of power that shook the very foundations of American democracy and left an indelible mark on the political landscape.

As the investigation unfolded, a tangled web of conspiracy began to unravel. The Nixon administration's attempts to obstruct justice were revealed through a series of shocking testimonies and leaked information. The infamous tape recordings of conversations in the Oval Office laid bare the lengths to which officials would go to conceal their misdeeds. The notion that the highest office in the land was embroiled in such nefarious activities fueled rampant speculation and distrust among the public, sparking debates that resonate even today about government integrity and the ethical limits of power.

But what made Watergate particularly intriguing was the involvement of various secretive organizations and the shadowy figures that flitted through the corridors of power. The scandal brought to light the influence of political operatives, lobbyists, and even the CIA, raising questions about the deep-seated connections between government and clandestine groups. This interplay of power dynamics not only fed conspiracy theories but also highlighted the vulnerabilities of democratic institutions when faced with entrenched interests willing to manipulate the system for personal gain.

Moreover, the media played a pivotal role in exposing the Watergate conspiracy, transforming investigative journalism into a powerful ally of the public. Reporters like Bob Woodward and Carl Bernstein became household names as they meticulously pieced together the puzzle, revealing the dark secrets that lay beneath the surface. Their relentless pursuit of truth not only led to the resignation of President Nixon but also galvanized a generation of journalists to hold those in power accountable, establishing a legacy that would inspire future whistleblowers and investigative efforts across various sectors.

The echoes of the Watergate Scandal are still felt today, serving as a potent reminder of the need for vigilance and skepticism in the face of authority. It has become a touchstone for discussions surrounding governmental transparency, ethical governance, and the potential for abuse of power. As conspiracy theories continue to swirl around contemporary political events, Watergate remains a cautionary tale, urging citizens to question, investigate, and demand accountability from those who govern. In a world where the shadows of history loom large, the lessons of Watergate remind us that the pursuit of truth is not just a noble endeavor but a necessary one for the health of any democracy.

The Iran-Contra Affair

The Iran-Contra Affair stands as one of the most audacious and controversial episodes in American political history, a perfect storm of intrigue that fuels conspiracy theories to this day. In the 1980s, as the Cold War cast a long shadow over global politics, the U.S. found itself entangled in a web of clandestine operations that would forever alter the landscape of government accountability. The scandal revolved around the Reagan administration's secret support for Contra rebels in Nicaragua, a move that violated both U.S. law and ethical standards. This covert operation, funded by the illegal sale of arms to Iran, a nation then deemed an enemy, raises fundamental questions about the limits of presidential power and the lengths to which a government might go to achieve its objectives.

At the heart of the Iran-Contra Affair lies a complex narrative filled with deception and betrayal. The Contras, opposing the Sandinista government in Nicaragua, were the beneficiaries of American aid despite Congress's prohibition of such support. In a twist that seems ripped from the pages of a political thriller, the Reagan administration sought to bypass legal restrictions by orchestrating a clandestine arms deal with Iran. The profits from these arms sales were then funneled to the Contras, creating a convoluted and illegal operation that thrived in the shadows. As the connections between these seemingly disparate events began to unravel, the American public was left grappling with the stark reality of their government's clandestine actions.

The fallout from the Iran-Contra Affair was nothing short of explosive, igniting a media frenzy and a fierce public debate over governmental integrity. Investigations revealed a web of deceit, with high-ranking officials, including National Security Advisor Oliver North, playing pivotal roles in orchestrating the operation. The subsequent hearings and investigations laid bare the lengths to which officials would go to protect their actions, raising alarms about accountability within the highest echelons of power. The revelations not only shook public confidence in government but also sparked conspiracy theories about hidden agendas and the true motivations behind these covert operations.

As the dust settled, the Iran-Contra Affair became emblematic of the broader issues of government transparency and accountability. It served as a catalyst for a generation of conspiracy theorists who questioned the narratives put forth by official sources. Was this merely a case of rogue operators acting beyond their authority, or was there a grander scheme at play? Theories abound, suggesting that this scandal was just one piece of a larger puzzle involving secret societies and shadowy organizations aiming to manipulate global politics for their own gain. Such speculation reflects a pervasive distrust in government, a sentiment that continues to resonate in the current political climate.

In examining the Iran-Contra Affair, one cannot help but recognize its enduring legacy in the realm of conspiracy theories. It serves not only as a historical lesson about the precarious balance between power and accountability but also as a reminder of the human tendency to seek hidden truths beneath the surface. As we delve into this shadowy chapter of history, it becomes evident that the Iran-Contra Affair is not merely a relic of the past; it continues to inspire questions about the integrity of our institutions and the unseen forces that shape our world, ensuring its place in the annals of conspiracy discourse for years to come.

Operation Paperclip

Operation Paperclip stands as one of the most intriguing and controversial covert operations in American history, illustrating the lengths to which governments will go to secure power and technological advancement. Following World War II, the United States faced a critical need to bolster its scientific and military capabilities amidst the growing tensions of the Cold War. Enter Operation Paperclip, a clandestine initiative that recruited over 1,600 German scientists, engineers, and technicians—many of whom had close ties to the Nazi regime. The operation was shrouded in secrecy, as the U.S. government sought to exploit the knowledge of these individuals while simultaneously burying their dark pasts, leading to a plethora of conspiracy theories surrounding the ethical implications of such actions.

The scientists brought to America through Operation Paperclip played pivotal roles in several critical areas, including aerospace, rocketry, and medicine. One of the most notable figures was Wernher von Braun, a former Nazi rocket engineer who became a key figure in the U.S. space program. His contributions helped propel the nation to the moon, yet his involvement with the Nazi regime raised uncomfortable questions about morality and accountability. Was the pursuit of technological superiority worth the moral compromises? This question continues to fuel debates among historians and conspiracy theorists alike, who argue over the possible repercussions of sheltering former Nazis in the name of progress.

As whispers about Operation Paperclip began to surface, the public's fascination with secretive government operations grew. This operation not only highlighted the complex relationship between science and politics but also underscored the potential for government cover-ups. The U.S. government's efforts to sanitize the backgrounds of these scientists, including the deletion of incriminating documents and the manipulation of their biographies, have led many to speculate about what else might have been hidden from the public eye. The notion that the government was willing to overlook heinous actions for the sake of technological advancement raises critical questions about transparency and trust in governmental institutions.

The legacy of Operation Paperclip extends beyond its immediate scientific achievements, intertwining with a broader narrative of conspiracy theories that continue to captivate imaginations. Many theorists speculate about the existence of secret societies that may have influenced the decision to recruit these scientists, positing that hidden agendas may have driven the U.S. government's choices. This intertwining of science, secrecy, and society has led to a rich tapestry of tales that explore the boundaries of ethics and ambition. The seductive idea that powerful groups manipulate events from behind the scenes only serves to deepen the allure of these narratives.

In today's context, the implications of Operation Paperclip resonate with ongoing discussions about ethics in science and technology. As we grapple with complex issues surrounding surveillance, medical advancements, and government transparency, the echoes of past operations remind us of the delicate balance between progress and morality. The saga of Operation Paperclip invites us to reflect on how far we are willing to go in the name of advancement and what we might be willing to overlook in the process. It serves as a cautionary tale, urging us to remain vigilant against the shadows that lurk in the corners of history, lest we find ourselves repeating the mistakes of the past.

Chapter 3: Celebrities and Their Secrets

The Death of Marilyn Monroe

The death of Marilyn Monroe on August 5, 1962, stands as one of the most enigmatic events in Hollywood history, igniting a firestorm of conspiracy theories that continue to captivate the imagination of many. Her demise, ruled a probable suicide by overdose, raised eyebrows from the outset. The circumstances surrounding her passing were shrouded in mystery, leading to rampant speculation about the involvement of powerful figures within the government, the entertainment industry, and even secret societies. The allure of Monroe's life and untimely death invites us into a labyrinth of intrigue that intertwines celebrity culture with the shadowy machinations of those in power.

One of the most prominent theories suggests that Monroe's relationship with President John F. Kennedy and his brother, Robert, placed her in a perilous position. Some believe that her knowledge of state secrets and her alleged involvement in a love triangle with the Kennedy brothers made her a liability. Could it be that her death was orchestrated to silence her? The theory posits that she was not merely a tragic figure but a pawn in a dangerous game played by the highest echelons of political power. The idea that a beloved icon could be sacrificed to protect the interests of those in authority sends chills down the spine and raises questions about the lengths to which powerful individuals might go to maintain their secrets.

Adding to the conspiracy is the peculiar behavior of those who surrounded Monroe in her final hours. Witnesses reported that her house was filled with strange characters, including individuals with ties to organized crime and political elites. The suggestion that Monroe's death was not just a personal tragedy but a calculated move by a coalition of influential players adds layers to the narrative. The fact that numerous key figures were present during her final moments gives rise to the unsettling possibility that her death was anything but an accident. The chaos and confusion surrounding the events of that night create fertile ground for speculation, leading many to question the official narrative.

Moreover, the involvement of medical professionals in Monroe's case has also come under scrutiny. Reports of discrepancies in the autopsy and the handling of her body raise significant questions about the integrity of the investigation. Some conspiracy theorists argue that the medical establishment may have been complicit in covering up the true nature of her death, perhaps to protect powerful interests that were threatened by her potential testimony or knowledge. This intersection of celebrity and medicine illustrates the troubling reality of how individuals can be manipulated by those with the means to control narratives, further complicating our understanding of Monroe's tragic end.

As we delve deeper into the shadows surrounding Marilyn Monroe's death, it becomes clear that the fascination with her story is not merely about a lost Hollywood starlet but represents a broader commentary on the interplay between celebrity, power, and conspiracy. Theories surrounding her demise reflect our anxieties about the unseen forces that govern our lives and the lengths to which individuals will go to conceal the truth. In a world where information is often obscured and manipulated, the legacy of Monroe's death challenges us to question the narratives we accept and to seek the hidden truths lurking beneath the surface of history.

The Elvis Presley Conspiracy

The world of celebrity has always been shrouded in mystery, but few figures have inspired as many conspiracy theories as Elvis Presley. The King of Rock and Roll, who captivated millions with his electrifying performances and magnetic personality, became an enigma after his untimely death in 1977. From claims of faked deaths to theories linking his demise to shadowy government agencies, the Elvis Presley conspiracy theories continue to thrive, capturing the imagination of fans and conspiracy enthusiasts alike. With each new revelation or rumor, the legend of Elvis only grows, inviting speculation and intrigue around his life and legacy.

One of the most prominent theories suggests that Elvis did not actually die but instead orchestrated an elaborate hoax to escape the pressures of fame. Proponents of this theory point to inconsistencies in the official narrative surrounding his death, such as the peculiar circumstances of his funeral and the missing coroner's report. This idea is fueled by alleged sightings of Elvis in various locations across the United States, with fans claiming to have encountered him in everything from small diners to major events. The allure of the King living in secrecy stimulates a fervent community of believers who hold steadfast to the notion that Elvis is out there, somewhere, enjoying life away from the spotlight.

Adding another layer to the conspiracy, some theorists propose that Elvis was targeted by government agencies due to his influence and the radical messages of his music. This theory suggests he may have been involved in a deeper political agenda, possibly as a pawn in the cultural battles of the 1960s and 1970s. The FBI reportedly kept tabs on him, viewing his popularity as a threat to the status quo. This intersection of celebrity and politics fuels speculation that his death could have been a result of government intervention, whether through coercion or more sinister means. Such narratives tap into the broader themes of distrust in authority and the belief that powerful entities manipulate those in the public eye.

The medical conspiracy theories surrounding Elvis's health and death also add to the mystique. Reports of his struggles with prescription drug addiction and obesity have led some to believe that his death was not merely a result of a heart attack but rather a cover-up for a larger health crisis. Skeptics of the official reports argue that medical professionals may have been complicit in obscuring the truth, raising questions about the pharmaceutical industry's role in the lives of celebrities. This theory resonates with broader fears regarding the medical establishment and the extent to which it may prioritize profit over patient care, especially for those in the limelight.

Ultimately, the Elvis Presley conspiracy theories illustrate a fascinating intersection of celebrity culture, historical context, and human psychology. The enduring nature of these theories reflects our collective desire to seek out hidden truths and understand the complexities of fame and legacy. Whether one believes that Elvis faked his death, was a victim of government machinations, or fell prey to the darker sides of fame, the discussions surrounding his life and untimely passing continue to provoke thought and fuel a vibrant community of conspiracy theorists. In a world where the truth often feels elusive, the legend of Elvis Presley serves as a reminder of the shadows lurking just beyond the surface of our understanding.

The Illuminati and Pop Culture

The Illuminati, a name that evokes intrigue and fascination, has
cemented its place in the annals of pop culture as a symbol of
hidden power and control. This secret society, often associated
with grand conspiracies and shadowy dealings, has become a
staple in movies, music, and literature. From Dan Brown's
thrilling novels to the captivating visuals of films like "The Da
Vinci Code," the portrayal of the Illuminati taps into our
collective anxieties about authority, surveillance, and the
unseen forces that shape our world. This cultural obsession not
only reflects our fears but also amplifies them, transforming
the Illuminati into a modern mythos that fuels conspiracy
theories and invites endless speculation.

In music, the influence of the Illuminati is palpable, with numerous artists being accused of affiliation with the society. From Jay-Z to Beyoncé, the symbolism embedded in lyrics, music videos, and public appearances has led fans to dissect every detail for hidden meanings. The use of all-seeing eyes, pyramids, and other esoteric imagery has sparked debates about whether these artists are mere entertainers or unwitting pawns in a grander scheme. This phenomenon illustrates how pop culture can both reflect and shape societal perceptions about power dynamics, challenging us to question who truly holds the reins of influence in the entertainment industry and beyond.

Television shows and documentaries have also contributed significantly to the mythos surrounding the Illuminati. Series like "The X-Files" and "American Horror Story" incorporate themes of secret societies and covert operations, captivating audiences through their blend of fiction and conspiracy. These narratives often serve as a commentary on real-world issues such as government surveillance and corporate greed, blurring the lines between entertainment and reality. By interweaving the enigmatic presence of the Illuminati into popular storylines, creators tap into a vein of paranoia that resonates deeply with viewers, encouraging them to consider the implications of hidden agendas in their own lives. Furthermore the internet age has transformed the way we engage with conspiracy theories about the illuminati. Social media platforms serve as breding grounds for discussions and theories, enabling individuals to connect over shared curiosities and suspicions. This democratization of information has led to the rapid spread of theories, often fueled by viral content and sensationalism. As influencers and content creators exploit the allure of the illuminati for views and engagement, the line between credible discourse and sensationalist conspiracy blurs, creating a complex tapestry of beliefs that challenges our understanding of truth in the digital age.

Ultimately, the Illuminati's integration into pop culture serves as a reflection of our society's deeper fears and questions about authority, knowledge, and control. Whether viewed through the lens of entertainment or as a catalyst for real-world discussions, the Illuminati embodies the age-old struggle against unseen powers. As audiences consume these narratives, they find themselves grappling with the implications of knowledge, secrecy, and agency in a world where the truth can often feel just out of reach. The enduring fascination with the Illuminati underscores a perpetual quest for understanding in an increasingly complex and interconnected world.

Chapter 4: Alien Encounters and UFO Sightings

Roswell: The Crash that Shook the World

The incident at Roswell in 1947 remains one of the most intriguing events in the annals of conspiracy theories, capturing the imagination of millions and fueling a plethora of speculations. An ordinary summer day turned extraordinary when reports emerged of a mysterious crash in the New Mexico desert. Initially described as a "flying disc" by the military, the narrative shifted almost overnight to a weather balloon. This sudden change in the official story triggered a whirlwind of theories, igniting public fascination with the possibility of extraterrestrial life and government cover-ups that have persisted for decades. The Roswell crash has since become a symbol of the broader struggle between the truth and the narratives constructed by those in power.

As the years rolled on, the Roswell incident evolved from a mere crash into a cornerstone of UFO lore. Eyewitness accounts began to surface, claiming to have seen unusual debris and even alien bodies at the crash site. These testimonies, often sensationalized, painted a picture of a government eager to hide its secrets from the public. Theories flourished, suggesting that the military not only recovered advanced technology but also engaged in a deliberate campaign to discredit witnesses and suppress information. This led to an ever-deepening divide between official narratives and the growing army of conspiracy theorists who believed that the truth was far stranger than fiction.

The implications of the Roswell crash reverberate beyond the realm of alien encounters; it serves as a lens through which we can examine the broader skepticism towards government institutions. The notion that a powerful entity could manipulate information to maintain control over the populace resonates with many who feel disenfranchised. This sentiment has been exacerbated by instances of proven cover-ups in various sectors, including politics, medicine, and finance. The Roswell incident stands as a pivotal moment that ignited a flame of distrust, leading to a greater questioning of not just the military, but all forms of authority.

What makes Roswell particularly compelling is its intersection with the culture of the time. The post-World War II era was ripe for conspiracy theories. The Cold War had instilled a pervasive fear of the unknown, and the public's thirst for knowledge about the universe was met with an equally strong desire to uncover hidden truths on Earth. The rise of science fiction in popular culture further fueled imaginations, making the idea of alien life not just plausible but desirable. This cultural backdrop ensured that Roswell would not merely be a footnote in history but a launchpad for an ongoing dialogue about existence, secrecy, and the nature of reality itself.

Today, as we sift through the layers of myth and fact surrounding Roswell, it is clear that the crash did more than shake the ground of New Mexico—it shook the very foundations of how we perceive truth and authority. The theories that emerged from that fateful day have not only persisted but have evolved, intertwining with various other conspiracy narratives that span from government surveillance to secret societies. This legacy continues to inspire new generations to question the status quo and search for answers in a world where the line between fact and fiction remains tantalizingly blurred. The crash at Roswell is more than just a story; it is a cultural phenomenon that challenges our understanding of history, truth, and the forces that shape our reality.

Area 51: Secrets of the Desert

Area 51, nestled deep within the Nevada desert, has long
captured the imagination of conspiracy theorists and curious
minds alike. This enigmatic military base, shrouded in secrecy,
is often at the center of discussions about extraterrestrial life
and advanced technologies. The very name evokes images of
UFO sightings, clandestine government experiments, and
shadowy figures conspiring in the night. For decades, the allure
of Area 51 has fueled speculation, creating a rich tapestry of
theories that challenge our understanding of reality and the
government's role in keeping the truth hidden.

The origins of Area 51 can be traced back to the Cold War era, when the U.S. government sought to develop advanced aircraft technology. However, the lack of transparency surrounding its operations gave rise to wild speculation. Was the government reverse-engineering alien spacecraft? Did they make contact with extraterrestrial beings? These questions have been pondered by enthusiasts, skeptics, and everyone in between. The allure of the unknown invites us to consider the possibility that our government has been hiding groundbreaking discoveries, perhaps even the existence of life beyond our planet.

Moreover, the secrecy surrounding Area 51 has been perpetuated by the government's own actions, including the use of aggressive tactics to discourage trespassing and the release of deliberately vague information. This behavior ignites the flames of suspicion and fuels an ever-growing narrative that something monumental is occurring behind those closed doors. The infamous 1997 incident involving the supposed retrieval of alien technology further cemented Area 51 as a focal point for conspiracy theories. The idea that our government might possess knowledge and artifacts from otherworldly sources is both thrilling and unsettling, making it a prime target for conspiracy theorists.

The cultural impact of Area 51 cannot be understated. It has permeated various aspects of popular culture, from films and television shows to literature and art. The intersection of fact and fiction in these portrayals only deepens the enigma surrounding the base. As stories of alien encounters and government cover-ups circulate, they create a narrative that compels individuals to question the very nature of truth. The concept of a secret society operating within the depths of the desert plays into our fears and fascinations, reminding us that there may be forces at play that we cannot comprehend or control.

Ultimately, Area 51 serves as a powerful symbol of our collective curiosity and distrust of authority. It embodies the spirit of inquiry that drives us to seek answers in a world often obscured by layers of deception. As we peel back the layers of history and conspiracy surrounding this iconic location, we are invited to confront not only the mysteries of the universe but also the complexities of our relationship with power and knowledge. The secrets of the desert may be elusive, but the quest for understanding continues to inspire and ignite the imagination of those willing to explore the shadows of history.

Modern-Day Sightings and Government Responses

In recent years, the landscape of conspiracy theories has been
invigorated by modern-day sightings of unexplained
phenomena and the responses—or lack thereof—from
governments around the world. This surge in interest can
largely be attributed to the advent of technology and social
media, which allow for rapid dissemination of information,
fostering a culture of skepticism toward official narratives.
Reports of unidentified flying objects (UFOs) have flooded news
feeds and social platforms, igniting discussions that span from
the extraterrestrial to the mundane. The implications of these
sightings stretch beyond mere curiosity, raising questions
about national security, transparency, and the very fabric of
reality itself.

The U.S. government's acknowledgment of UFOs, rebranded as Unidentified Aerial Phenomena (UAP), has further fueled public intrigue. In 2020, the Pentagon established the Unidentified Aerial Phenomena Task Force, a significant step that many conspiracy enthusiasts interpret as an admission of the existence of otherworldly visitors. The release of previously classified videos showing encounters between military pilots and UAPs only intensified speculation about what the government knows and is not telling us. This newfound openness, however, has not quelled the conspiracy theories; instead, it has paved the way for even more elaborate narratives, including those involving secret government experiments and cover-ups that span decades.

Moreover, the responses from various governments worldwide have varied dramatically, revealing a patchwork of secrecy and openness that fuels conspiracy theories. In countries like Brazil and the UK, officials have released documents regarding UFO sightings, ostensibly to promote transparency. However, the selective release of information often leads to skepticism rather than trust.

Critics argue that they are still withholding significant data, creating a fertile ground for conspiracy theorists who suggest that these sightings are linked to broader, more sinister agendas, including surveillance technologies and mind control experiments.

Celebrity involvement in these conspiracy narratives adds another layer of complexity and excitement. Influential figures often share their own encounters or beliefs about UFOs, secret societies, and government cover-ups, amplifying the allure of these theories. When a high-profile individual speaks out, it can lend an air of legitimacy to otherwise fringe ideas. This phenomenon illustrates how the intersection of fame and conspiracy can captivate public attention, leading to increased scrutiny of government actions and the institutions that underpin society. The blending of celebrity culture with conspiracy theories creates a unique environment where the boundaries of reality and fiction blur, leaving many questioning what is true.

As we navigate this intricate web of modern-day sightings and government responses, it becomes increasingly clear that the quest for truth is far from over. The excitement surrounding UFOs, secret societies, and government transparency continues to inspire both fervent belief and deep skepticism. Each new sighting or revelation serves as a catalyst for further inquiry, inviting individuals to delve deeper into the shadows of history. In this era of information overload, where every theory can find its audience, the challenge remains: discerning fact from fiction in a world where the truth may be stranger than we can imagine.

Chapter 5: The Dark World of Secret Societies

The Freemasons: Myths and Realities

The Freemasons have long been the subject of fascination and intrigue, often appearing in the realm of conspiracy theories as a shadowy force influencing global events. Myths surrounding this secretive organization abound, suggesting that its members wield disproportionate power over governments, economies, and societal structures. From whispered tales of ancient rituals to claims of a grand conspiracy to control the world, the narrative surrounding the Freemasons is rich with sensationalism. Yet, as we delve deeper into the realities of this organization, it becomes evident that the truth is often far less sensational than the myths that surround it.

Shadows of History: Unraveling the Great Conspiracy Theories of Our Time

At its core, the Freemasons are a fraternal organization that traces its origins back to the late 16th and early 17th centuries. Initially formed as a guild for stonemasons, the organization gradually evolved, inviting members from various professions and backgrounds. The Masonic philosophy is grounded in principles of brotherhood, charity, and moral uprightness, offering a space for camaraderie and personal growth. While the secretive nature of their meetings has fueled speculation, many of their values, such as community service and ethical conduct, are commendable and publicly promoted.

Despite the positive aspects of Freemasonry, the myths persist, often amplified by a lack of understanding. Some conspiracy theorists posit that the Freemasons are a puppet master controlling world events from behind the scenes. This notion is further fueled by the presence of notable historical figures among their ranks, including politicians, military leaders, and influential thinkers. Yet, it is crucial to differentiate between the individual beliefs and actions of Masons and the organization itself. Many members engage in their local lodges without any grand agenda, focused instead on fellowship and charitable work, rather than manipulating global affairs.

Shadows of History: Unraveling the Great Conspiracy Theories of Our Time

The allure of Freemasonry in the context of conspiracy theories often leads to the conflation of unrelated events and individuals into a narrative of control and secrecy. For example, the frequent association of Freemasons with other secret societies, such as the Illuminati, creates an impression of a vast interconnected web of influence. However, many historians argue that the two organizations are distinct, with differing purposes and philosophies. The intertwining of these narratives often results in a convoluted understanding of both groups, obscuring the true nature of their activities and goals.

Ultimately, while the myths surrounding the Freemasons can be captivating, it is essential to approach them with a critical eye. The realities of the organization reveal a complex tapestry of history, culture, and human connection that transcends the simplistic narratives often presented in popular media. By recognizing the distinction between myth and reality, we can appreciate the Freemasons not as shadowy puppeteers but as a collective of individuals who have sought to foster community and personal development throughout history, albeit under the veil of secrecy that invites speculation and curiosity.

The Illuminati: Power and Influence

The Illuminati, a term that conjures images of shadowy figures pulling the strings behind the scenes, has captivated the imagination of conspiracy theorists and historians alike. This clandestine group, often linked to the Enlightenment-era Bavarian Illuminati, is said to wield immense power and influence over global events. The allure of the Illuminati lies not only in its mysterious origins but also in its purported ability to shape political landscapes, control economies, and even manipulate cultural trends. As we delve into the depths of this enigma, we uncover the threads connecting the Illuminati to various conspiracy theories that have permeated our society.

At the heart of many conspiracy theories is the belief that the Illuminati operates as a secret society with a singular agenda: to establish a New World Order. This concept suggests that a small elite group seeks to control world governments, economies, and even societies, all while remaining hidden from public scrutiny. Proponents of this theory argue that major political decisions are not made through democratic processes but rather orchestrated by influential members of this secretive organization. The idea that powerful figures, including politicians and business magnates, might be part of this grand design fuels speculation and paranoia, prompting individuals to scrutinize the motives behind global decisions.

The influence of the Illuminati extends beyond the political realm, seeping into entertainment and popular culture. Celebrities are often implicated in these theories, accused of being pawns or even high-ranking members of the Illuminati. From musicians who incorporate esoteric symbols in their music videos to actors rumored to participate in secret rituals, the narrative suggests a pervasive control over the entertainment industry. This phenomenon not only reflects society's fascination with fame but also raises questions about the extent to which public figures may be manipulated by unseen forces. The intersection of celebrity culture and Illuminati conspiracy theories reveals a cultural anxiety about the motivations and influences that shape our perceptions of fame and success.

As we explore the financial implications of the Illuminati, we encounter claims that this secret society exerts control over global markets and economies. Conspiracy theorists argue that financial crises, stock market fluctuations, and even the rise and fall of currencies are all orchestrated events designed to maintain the elite's grip on power. The belief that a select group of individuals can manipulate economic systems fosters distrust in traditional institutions and banking systems, leading to a growing skepticism about the transparency of financial dealings. This narrative is particularly appealing in times of economic uncertainty, as it provides a scapegoat for the complexities of a global economy that often feels beyond the average person's control.

Technological advancements have also become entwined with the narrative of the Illuminati, as the rise of surveillance and data collection fuels fears of an omnipresent control system. With the advent of social media and smart devices, the potential for monitoring and manipulating public opinion has never been greater. Conspiracy theorists argue that the Illuminati uses technology to surveil citizens, influencing behavior and thoughts on a massive scale. This intersection of technology and conspiracy highlights a growing concern about privacy and autonomy in a world where information is both a tool and a weapon. As we navigate through this digital landscape, the specter of the Illuminati looms large, prompting us to question who truly holds the reins of power in our increasingly interconnected lives.

Ultimately, the Illuminati symbolizes our collective anxieties about power, control, and the unknown forces that shape our world. Whether viewed as a genuine threat or a figment of imagination, the idea of a secret society pulling strings from the shadows resonates deeply within the human psyche. As we continue to unravel the threads of history, the Illuminati serves as a powerful reminder of our need to seek answers in an age rife with uncertainty and complexity. In exploring this phenomenon, we not only delve into the nature of conspiracy theories but also reflect on the broader implications of trust, authority, and the quest for truth in a world that can often feel bewildering.

Other Notable Secret Organizations

Throughout history, the existence of secret organizations has sparked intrigue and speculation, often becoming the backbone of conspiracy theories that capture our imagination. One of the most notable among these is the Illuminati, a name that evokes images of shadowy figures manipulating world events from behind the scenes. Originally founded in the 18th century, the Bavarian Illuminati aimed to promote Enlightenment ideals. However, its alleged infiltration into various sectors, including government and finance, has given rise to countless theories suggesting that they continue to exert control over global affairs. This blend of historical fact and myth fuels the belief that a hidden cabal remains active today, shaping our world in ways we can only begin to fathom.

Another intriguing group is the Freemasons, whose origins date back to the late 16th century. Often shrouded in mystery and ritual, the Freemasons have been linked to various political and social movements throughout history. Their secretive nature has led many to speculate about their influence on critical events, from the American Revolution to the French Revolution. Despite their philanthropic endeavors, conspiracy theorists argue that the Masonic brotherhood operates with a hidden agenda, aiming to establish a new world order. This perception continues to thrive, as the Freemasons are frequently portrayed as puppeteers orchestrating the actions of influential figures in society.

Moving into the realm of modern conspiracies, the Bilderberg Group stands out as an elite assembly of political leaders, business magnates, and intellectuals. Founded in 1954, this annual conference is often criticized for its lack of transparency and media coverage. Conspiracy theorists argue that the clandestine meetings serve as a breeding ground for policies that shape global economics and politics without public consent. The allure of the Bilderberg Group lies in its exclusivity, leading many to believe that it holds the keys to understanding the machinations of global governance. This perception fuels fears about the erosion of democracy and the rise of technocratic control, as discussions behind closed doors could very well dictate the future of nations.

In the realm of celebrity conspiracy theories, the Church of Scientology has garnered significant attention. Founded by L. Ron Hubbard in the 1950s, Scientology is often described as a religion, but many critics view it as a secretive organization with a questionable agenda. Accusations of manipulation, abuse, and cover-ups within the church have led to widespread scrutiny and speculation. The belief that Scientology wields considerable power over its members and the media has ignited discussions about the lengths organizations will go to maintain control and silence dissenting voices. This aspect of conspiracy theory underscores our fascination with the intersection of fame, power, and secrecy.

Lastly, the enigmatic nature of the Rosicrucians cannot be overlooked. This mystical organization, which emerged in the early 17th century, claims to possess ancient wisdom and esoteric knowledge. Often associated with alchemy and spiritual enlightenment, the Rosicrucians have been linked to various conspiracy theories regarding their influence on science, religion, and politics. The allure of their purported hidden knowledge captivates those who seek to uncover the secrets of the universe. As we delve deeper into the fabric of these organizations, it becomes evident that the intersection of secrecy and power continues to fuel our fascination with conspiracy theories, challenging us to question the narratives that shape our understanding of history and reality.

Chapter 6: Medical and Pharmaceutical Conspiracies

The Vaccine Debate: Myths and Facts

The vaccine debate stands as one of the most contentious issues in contemporary society, fueled by a blend of science, emotion, and misinformation. Myths surrounding vaccines have proliferated, often overshadowing the robust scientific evidence supporting their efficacy and safety. It is crucial to dissect these myths, not only to illuminate the truth but to understand how they fit into the broader tapestry of conspiracy theories that have historically shaped public perception. From the idea that vaccines cause autism to claims of government control through inoculation, these narratives can evoke fear and skepticism, illustrating the powerful impact of misinformation in shaping societal beliefs.

One prevalent myth is the assertion that vaccines are primarily a profit-driven endeavor for pharmaceutical companies. While it is true that the medical industry is lucrative, the development and distribution of vaccines are heavily regulated and supported by scientific research. Vaccination programs have historically led to the eradication of diseases like smallpox and significant reductions in polio cases. This myth often intertwines with broader conspiracy theories about government and corporate collusion, suggesting that the public is being manipulated for profit rather than being protected from disease. Yet, the public health successes attributed to vaccines tell a different story—one of collaboration, scientific advancement, and community health.

Another myth that deserves attention is the belief that vaccines contain harmful substances that can compromise health. This notion has been perpetuated by selective interpretations of vaccine ingredients, often taken out of context to stoke fear. In truth, vaccines undergo rigorous testing to ensure their safety. The ingredients, such as adjuvants and preservatives, are present in quantities deemed safe by health authorities. By understanding the science behind these components, adults can better navigate the complex landscape of vaccine misinformation. This knowledge not only dispels myths but also reinforces the importance of informed decision-making based on facts rather than fear.

The role of media and social networks cannot be overlooked in this vaccine debate. In an age where information travels at lightning speed, the spread of conspiracy theories and myths often outpaces factual discourse. Social media platforms have become breeding grounds for sensationalism, where anecdotal evidence can overshadow empirical research. This dynamic leads to an environment where myths thrive, creating echo chambers that reinforce misconceptions. Understanding the mechanics of information dissemination allows adults to critically evaluate sources and encourages a more discerning approach to health-related content, ultimately fostering a culture of inquiry rather than blind acceptance.

Addressing the vaccine debate requires an enthusiastic commitment to education and dialogue. Engaging with the community to debunk myths and share factual information creates a foundation for informed decision-making. By emphasizing the collective benefits of vaccination—community immunity, reduced healthcare costs, and the preservation of public health—we can counterbalance the fear and suspicion that often accompany conspiracy theories. The vaccine debate is more than a health issue; it reflects our ability to confront and navigate the complexities of information in an era dominated by conspiracy theories, misinformation, and a yearning for truth.

Big Pharma: Profits Over People?

The pharmaceutical industry, often referred to as "Big Pharma." has long been a focal point of intense scrutiny and conspiracy theories. Critics argue that the industry's relentless pursuit of profit cones at the expense of public health and ethical responsibility. From questionable marketing practices to the manipulation of drug pricing, the narrative that Big Pharma prioritizes profits over people has gained traction, leaving many to wonder if the health of the population is genuinely at the forefront of pharmaceutical companies' missions or merely a vehicle for financial gain.

At the heart of this debate lies the staggering cost of prescription medications, which continues to rise at an alarming rate. Many believe that the exorbitant prices reflect not just the research and development costs but also the industry's willingness to exploit patients' needs. The notion that life-saving drugs are priced out of reach for countless individuals raises critical questions about the motives driving these corporations. Is it truly about innovation and improving health outcomes, or is it a calculated strategy to maximize profitability, even if it means sacrificing accessibility for millions?

Furthermore, allegations of collusion between pharmaceutical companies and regulatory bodies have fueled suspicions of a grand conspiracy at play. The revolving door between industry and government positions has led to a perception that regulatory agencies may prioritize corporate interests over public welfare. Instances where questionable clinical trial results are swept under the rug or manipulated to favor new drugs only intensify the doubts. This perceived lack of transparency has birthed a myriad of theories suggesting that the very institutions meant to safeguard public health might be complicit in a larger scheme to bolster the pharmaceutical industry's bottom line.

The narrative extends beyond pricing and regulatory issues. The opioid crisis serves as a glaring example of how profit motives can lead to catastrophic consequences. Pharmaceutical companies aggressively marketed opioids, downplaying their addictive potential in pursuit of market dominance. The aftermath has been devastating, resulting in widespread addiction and loss of life. This tragedy has led many to question the ethical boundaries of pharmaceutical marketing and the extent to which profit drives the decisions that impact public health on such a monumental scale.

In a world where the line between health and profitability is increasingly blurred, the conversation surrounding Big Pharma is more crucial than ever. As consumers become more informed and skeptical of the pharmaceutical narrative, the call for accountability grows louder. The clash between public health and corporate profit continues to ignite passionate debates, leaving us with a lingering question: can we trust that our health is a priority for those who wield such immense power, or are we merely pawns in a game dictated by profit margins? The shadows of history reveal a complex interplay of greed, ethics, and the health of the populace—a narrative that demands our attention and scrutiny.

Historical Medical Cover-Ups

The annals of history are rife with instances where medical
practices and discoveries have been shrouded in secrecy or
manipulated for ulterior motives. From the infamous Tuskegee
Syphilis Study, where African American men were deliberately
left untreated to study the progression of the disease, to the
covert testing of LSD on unsuspecting military personnel, these
cover-ups reveal a darker side of medical ethics. These events
raise unsettling questions about the trustworthiness of
institutions that are supposed to safeguard public health. As we
delve into these historical medical cover-ups, we unveil layers
of deception that challenge our understanding of integrity in
medicine.

One cannot overlook the role of government in these conspiracies. The Tuskegee Study, conducted by the U.S. Public Health Service from the 1930s to the 1970s, is a glaring example of how the government exploited vulnerable populations under the guise of research. The participants were misled, led to believe they were receiving free healthcare, while the reality was far more sinister. This betrayal ignited outrage and has since fueled distrust in public health systems, echoing through generations. The implications of such cover-ups extend far beyond the individuals involved, creating a ripple effect of skepticism toward medical advancements and government oversight.

Shadows of History: Unraveling the Great Conspiracy Theories of Our Time

In the realm of celebrity, the manipulation of health narratives can have profound impacts on public perception. The case of a famous pop star who allegedly underwent a secretive medical procedure to enhance her career speaks volumes about the intersection of fame and health. Rumors suggest that certain celebrities have been privy to exclusive medical technologies or treatments, raising eyebrows and prompting speculation about the lengths to which the elite will go to maintain their status. These hidden narratives not only shape public opinion but also reflect broader societal issues regarding access to healthcare and the ethics of treatment disparities.

Alien and UFO conspiracies have also intersected with medical cover-ups, particularly in the context of alleged government experiments. The Roswell incident in 1947, where an unidentified object crashed in New Mexico, is often linked to stories of secret medical experimentation on extraterrestrial beings. While many dismiss these tales as mere fiction, they tap into a collective anxiety surrounding the unknown and the potential for government manipulation. The idea that advanced medical technologies or knowledge could be hidden away from the public, potentially derived from extraterrestrial sources, ignites the imagination and stirs the pot of conspiracy theories.

As we sift through the shadows of these historical medical cover-ups, it becomes increasingly clear that the implications are vast. The intertwining of government interests, celebrity influence, and the fascination with the unknown create a fertile ground for conspiracy theories to flourish. Each revelation serves as a reminder that the quest for truth in the medical field is often obscured by layers of intrigue and deception. Understanding these historical narratives allows us to critically assess the present and advocate for transparency in healthcare, ensuring that the lessons of the past pave the way for a more ethical future.

Chapter 7: Financial and Economic Conspiracies

The 2008 Financial Crisis: A Setup?

The 2008 financial crisis stands as one of the most significant economic upheavals in modern history, shaking the foundations of global finance and igniting a firestorm of conspiracy theories. Many believe that this catastrophic event was not merely a result of market forces but rather a meticulously orchestrated setup. The narrative that emerges from this perspective suggests that powerful elites, driven by greed and a thirst for control, manipulated the financial system to serve their interests while leaving the average citizen to bear the brunt of the fallout. This backdrop of betrayal and manipulation raises questions about the integrity of the institutions we rely on and the unseen hands that may have guided economic policy in the years leading up to the crisis.

As we delve deeper into the circumstances surrounding the financial collapse, it's essential to consider the role of subprime mortgages. Financial institutions, eager for profit, packaged these high-risk loans into complex securities that were sold worldwide. This deceptive practice not only masked the underlying risk but also laid the groundwork for the eventual meltdown. Critics argue that regulatory bodies were either oblivious or complicit in allowing such practices to proliferate. Could it be that these regulators were, in fact, puppets of a larger scheme designed to enrich the elite at the expense of the common man? The timing of the crisis, coinciding with significant political shifts and the rise of certain financial powerhouses, has fueled speculation that the entire event was premeditated.

The government's response to the crisis further complicates
the narrative. The Troubled Asset Relief Program (TARP) was
introduced to stabilize the financial system, but many viewed it
as a bailout for the rich while the average citizen suffered. The
infusion of taxpayer money into failing banks raised eyebrows
and led to a growing sentiment that the government was not
acting in the best interests of its people. This perception of
betrayal has given rise to theories suggesting that the crisis was
a deliberate act to consolidate power among financial elites and
fortify their grip on the economy. The subsequent lack of
accountability for those responsible only deepened the distrust
in governmental institutions, fostering a breeding ground for
conspiracy theories.

Moreover, the aftermath of the crisis saw a significant increase in surveillance and control measures under the guise of economic stability. The argument could be made that the financial crisis was an opportunity for governments to expand their powers, implementing policies that encroached upon personal freedoms. This notion aligns with various conspiracy theories suggesting that significant events are often exploited by those in power to tighten their grip on society. The intertwining of economic turmoil with heightened surveillance creates a chilling narrative that raises questions about freedom, privacy, and the lengths to which authorities will go to maintain control.

In conclusion, the 2008 financial crisis serves as a potent reminder of the fragility of our economic systems and the potential for manipulation by those in power. The theories surrounding this monumental event challenge us to examine the motives behind the actions of financial institutions and government entities. As we explore these shadows of history, it becomes clear that the intersection of financial crises and conspiracy theories is not merely an academic exercise; it is a crucial lens through which we can better understand the complexities of power, control, and the ongoing struggle for justice in a world rife with hidden agendas.

The Role of Central Banks

Central banks play a pivotal role in shaping the economic landscape, often surrounded by an air of mystery that fuels conspiracy theories. These institutions are tasked with regulating monetary policy, controlling inflation, and managing the country's currency. Yet, beneath their official mandates lies a world of speculation and intrigue. Many conspiracy theorists argue that central banks operate as shadowy entities, pulling the strings of global finance and exerting undue influence over governments. This perception is not without merit, as the decisions made by central banks can have profound implications for the economy, leading to questions about who truly benefits from their actions.

The Federal Reserve in the United States, for instance, has often been at the center of heated debate. Critics suggest that the Fed is not merely a governmental body but rather an extension of powerful private interests, including international banking families and elite financiers. This notion has given rise to a plethora of conspiracy theories, suggesting that economic crises are orchestrated to consolidate wealth and power among a select few. The belief that central banks manipulate interest rates and currency values to serve their own ends resonates with those who view economic downturns not as natural phenomena but as intentional acts designed to control the masses.

Moreover, the secretive nature of central bank meetings and decisions can stoke the flames of suspicion. The lack of transparency surrounding monetary policy decisions leads many to speculate about what is truly being discussed behind closed doors. Are these meetings where decisions are made that prioritize the interests of the elite over the common citizen? The idea that central banks are involved in covert operations to stabilize or destabilize economies for geopolitical advantage is a fertile ground for conspiracy theorists, who argue that the public is rarely informed of the real agendas at play.

In addition to economic manipulation, central banks are also connected to larger narratives about surveillance and control. The advent of digital currencies and the push for cashless societies have raised concerns about privacy and government oversight. Many theorists suggest that central banks are not just institutions of monetary policy but are also at the forefront of a broader agenda to monitor and control individual financial behaviors. This perspective aligns with fears about government overreach and the loss of personal autonomy in an increasingly digitized world.

Ultimately, the role of central banks transcends mere economic management; it intertwines with the very fabric of societal trust and governance. As they navigate the complexities of modern economies, central banks must also contend with the shadows of conspiracy theories that challenge their legitimacy. This intersection of finance and speculation highlights the ongoing struggle for transparency and accountability in institutions that wield significant power over our lives. The intrigue surrounding central banks serves as a reminder of the delicate balance between authority and skepticism, inviting us to question how much we really know about the forces shaping our world.

Globalization and Economic Manipulation

Globalization has become a defining characteristic of our era,
intertwining economies, cultures, and societies across the
globe. However, beneath this surface of interconnectedness lies
a complex web of economic manipulation that fuels
speculation and conspiracy theories. Many believe that
powerful entities leverage globalization to exert control over
nations and individuals, creating a shadow economy that
operates outside the bounds of ethical standards. From
multinational corporations to secretive financial institutions,
the narrative of globalization often raises questions about who
truly benefits and who suffers in this intricate dance of capital
and influence. At the heart of this discussion is the role of
international organizations such as the International Monetary
Fund and the World Bank. These institutions, often perceived as
benevolent forces for development, are frequently accused of
imposing stringent conditions on loans that serve to entrench
the power of the elites while crippling local economies. Critics
argue that this dynamic leads to a form of economic
imperialism, where the interests of a few dictate the fates of
many. This perspective fuels the belief that globalization is not
merely an economic

phenomenon but a strategic maneuver for the elite to maintain their dominance over global resources and labor.

Moreover, the rise of multinational corporations has given these entities unprecedented power to shape markets and consumer behavior worldwide. With their vast resources, these corporations can manipulate supply chains to their advantage, often at the expense of smaller competitors and local businesses. This creates an environment ripe for conspiracy theories, as individuals wonder whether these giants collude to stifle innovation and maintain control over entire industries. The idea that a handful of corporations can dictate global economic trends leads many to suspect that there are hidden agendas at play, further feeding the flames of conspiracy thinking.

Celebrity conspiracy theories also intersect with globalization, as public figures often become unwitting pawns in the economic game. The manipulation of celebrity personas by media conglomerates can lead to the perception that these individuals are mere distractions, designed to divert attention from more significant global issues. The intertwining of celebrity culture and economic power raises intriguing questions about who is truly pulling the strings. Are celebrities used as tools for larger economic manipulations, or do they, too, fall victim to the very systems they seem to represent? This duality adds layers to the conspiracy narrative, making it all the more compelling for the public.

Finally, as technology evolves, so too does the potential for surveillance and control under the guise of globalization. With the advent of digital currencies and the increasing influence of tech giants on economic systems, conspiracy theorists argue that the global financial landscape is more susceptible to manipulation than ever before. The confluence of surveillance technology and economic power raises alarms about privacy, autonomy, and the potential for dystopian futures. In this context, globalization is not just a benign process of integration; it becomes a battleground for control, where economic manipulation is but one of many strategies employed by those in the shadows.

Chapter 8: Technology and Surveillance Conspiracies

The Rise of Big Tech

The rise of big tech is not just a chapter in the annals of modern history; it is a seismic shift that has shaped our society in ways that are both profound and unsettling. As technology companies have surged to unprecedented power and influence, they have raised an array of questions that echo through the corridors of conspiracy theory: Who truly controls these giants? What hidden agendas lie behind their innovations? In the shadows of Silicon Valley, the intertwining of technology, politics, and finance has birthed a new landscape where transparency seems to vanish, and the public's trust hangs precariously in the balance.

From the dawn of the internet to the omnipresence of smartphones, big tech has transformed communication, commerce, and even our very perception of reality. However, as these companies grew, so did concerns about their reach into our lives. Surveillance capitalism, a term that has gained traction in recent years, encapsulates the fear that personal data is being harvested and weaponized against individuals. This notion has given rise to conspiracy theories suggesting that these corporations, in collusion with government entities, are not merely observing us but actively manipulating our thoughts and behaviors for profit and control.

The connection between big tech and government has often been likened to a symbiotic relationship where both entities benefit at the expense of the individual. Leaks and whistleblower accounts, from the likes of Edward Snowden, have unveiled the murky waters of surveillance programs that intertwine with tech giants. Such revelations have fostered a fertile ground for conspiracy theorists who argue that these companies are unwittingly—or perhaps willingly—agents of a larger governmental agenda, leading us down a path of digital authoritarianism under the guise of convenience and security.

In the realm of celebrity and culture, this dynamic takes on a different hue. The intersection of big tech and celebrity culture has spawned its own set of conspiracy theories, where influencers and public figures are seen as pawns in a grand game orchestrated by tech moguls. The idea that these personalities are being used to shape public perception and distract from more sinister activities has led many to question the authenticity of the very content they consume. As social media platforms dictate trends, the underlying question remains: who is truly in control of the narrative?

Finally, as concerns mount over the environmental impact of tech giants and their relentless pursuit of growth, a new breed of conspiracy theory has emerged. Critics argue that big tech's innovations often mask deeper ecological issues, suggesting that the pursuit of profit is prioritized over the planet's well-being. This has led to speculation that major corporations are not only contributing to environmental degradation but are also engaged in cover-ups to hide the true costs of their operations. As we delve deeper into the shadows of history, the rise of big tech presents a complex tapestry of power, control, and the ever-elusive truth that continues to fuel the fires of conspiracy theories in our time.

Privacy vs. Security: The Great Debate

In the heart of contemporary discourse lies the electrifying clash between privacy and security, a debate that echoes through the annals of history and reverberates in every corner of our society. The tension between individual rights and collective safety has fueled countless conspiracy theories, from government surveillance programs to hidden agendas orchestrated by secret societies. As we peel back the layers of this complex issue, we discover that the battle for privacy is not just a modern phenomenon but a timeless struggle, punctuated by moments of intense paranoia and suspicion. Each era's technological advancements have repeatedly sparked fears of encroachment on personal freedoms, leading to a fertile ground for conspiracy theories to flourish.

Consider the chilling implications of surveillance technologies that have become ubiquitous in our lives. The advent of the internet, smartphones, and smart devices has ushered in an age of unprecedented connectivity, but it has also raised alarm bells regarding governmental overreach. The revelations of whistleblowers like Edward Snowden unveiled a shadowy world of mass data collection, prompting citizens to question the true cost of their safety. Are we trading our privacy for the illusion of security? This question has ignited a firestorm of debate, driving many to dive deep into the murky waters of conspiracy theories, where the government is often depicted as a puppet master, pulling strings behind a veil of secrecy.

The world of celebrity conspiracies also provides a fascinating lens through which to examine this dichotomy. The public's obsession with the lives of the rich and famous often leads to wild theories about their actions being manipulated by powerful elites. Whether it's claims of mind control by secret societies or elaborate cover-ups surrounding celebrity deaths, these narratives underscore a profound distrust of authority. Fans become detectives, piecing together fragments of information and signals, convinced that the truth is hidden just beneath the surface. In these stories, the struggle for privacy emerges not only for the individuals in the spotlight but also for the masses who feel their own rights are under siege.

As we delve into the realm of medical and pharmaceutical conspiracies, the tension intensifies further. The COVID-19 pandemic brought these issues to the forefront, with debates raging over vaccine efficacy, government mandates, and the role of pharmaceutical companies. Many have posited that health data is being weaponized in the name of security, leading to a belief that the healthcare system is riddled with nefarious motives. Conspiracies abound, suggesting that profit motives overshadow public health, and in this landscape, the battle for privacy takes on a life-or-death urgency. The distrust of institutions fuels a desire for transparency, and the stakes become higher as individuals grapple with the implications of surrendering their personal information.

Finally, the political arena serves as a battleground where privacy and security collide with dramatic intensity. The rise of authoritarian regimes often correlates with increased surveillance and diminished civil liberties, igniting fears of a dystopian future. Political conspiracy theories thrive in this environment, as citizens question the integrity of their leaders and the motives behind their policies. The idea that governments manipulate crises to justify invasive security measures resonates deeply, leading to widespread skepticism. As we explore these intertwined narratives, it becomes clear that the debate over privacy and security is not merely an academic exercise; it is a clarion call for vigilance and awareness.

The shadows of history remind us that while the quest for safety is legitimate, it must never come at the cost of our fundamental rights.

Social Media and Information Control

Social media has revolutionized the way information is disseminated and consumed, creating a digital landscape where conspiracy theories can flourish. With the click of a button, narratives that challenge the mainstream can spread like wildfire, often eclipsing factual reporting. This phenomenon has become particularly pronounced in the realms of historical conspiracy theories and government cover-ups, where platforms like Twitter and Facebook serve as battlegrounds for competing narratives. Users, emboldened by anonymity and the viral nature of content, can amplify their beliefs while creating echo chambers that reinforce their views. This dynamic raises critical questions about the nature of truth in our society and the role of social media as both a facilitator and a gatekeeper of information.

In the world of celebrity conspiracy theories, social media acts as a double-edged sword. On one hand, it allows fans to engage with their idols and share their thoughts; on the other, it provides a fertile ground for misinformation. Rumors about celebrity deaths, secret relationships, and hidden lives can gain traction almost overnight, often with little to no basis in fact. The allure of the sensational captures attention and drives engagement, leading to a cycle where the absurd becomes believable, and the public's appetite for scandal overshadows the pursuit of truth. Platforms that thrive on sensationalism can distort our perceptions of reality, making it increasingly difficult to separate fact from fiction in the lives of those we idolize.

Shadows of History: Unraveling the Great Conspiracy Theories of Our Time

Alien and UFO conspiracies have found a resurgence in the age of social media, where enthusiasts share sightings, theories, and alleged government cover-ups with unparalleled ease. Videos purporting to show extraterrestrial crafts or secretive military maneuvers circulate widely, often garnering millions of views. This viral potential can lead to the solidification of certain beliefs, even in the face of contradictory evidence. The interplay between social media and these conspiracies often fuels a sense of community among believers, creating a network of support that can be incredibly persuasive. As narratives about alien encounters intertwine with broader themes of surveillance and government secrecy, the implications for public discourse are profound and far-reaching.

Secret societies and organizations, long the subject of intrigue and speculation, have also found their place within the digital realm. Social media platforms provide a stage for theorists to propose connections between high-profile figures and shadowy groups, often linking historical events to these clandestine organizations. The accessibility of information, combined with the ease of sharing, allows for a rapid proliferation of theories that can alter public perception and influence societal beliefs. As users engage with these narratives, they often become unwitting participants in a larger game of perception versus reality, where the lines between fact and fiction become increasingly blurred.

Finally, the intersection of medical and pharmaceutical conspiracies with social media illustrates how misinformation can have tangible consequences for public health. During times of crisis, such as the COVID-19 pandemic, false information about vaccines and treatments spread rapidly, fueled by fear and distrust. Social media platforms grapple with moderating this content, often facing criticism for either censorship or inaction. The consequences of these dynamics extend beyond individual beliefs; they can shape public policy and influence societal behavior. As we navigate this complex landscape, the challenge remains to discern the truth amid the cacophony of voices, ensuring that the shadows of conspiracy do not obscure the light of reasoned discourse.

Chapter 9: Political Conspiracy Theories

Assassinations: Truth or Cover-Up?

Assassinations have long been a focal point for conspiracy theorists, igniting imaginations and fueling debates about the hidden machinations of powerful entities. From the tragic shooting of President John F. Kennedy to the untimely demise of influential figures like Martin Luther King Jr. and Robert F. Kennedy, these events are often clouded by speculation and whispers of cover-ups. The allure of these conspiracies lies in their potential to reveal deeper truths about the political climate of their times and the lengths to which individuals or organizations will go to maintain control or eliminate threats to their power.

Exploring the assassination of JFK, it becomes evident how quickly a straightforward narrative can dissolve into a web of intrigue. Official accounts suggest a lone gunman, Lee Harvey Oswald, acted alone, but countless theories challenge this, proposing everything from government involvement to the mafia's hand in the plot. The sheer volume of books, documentaries, and discussions surrounding this single event highlights a thirst for understanding that seems unquenchable. Is the truth hidden beneath layers of government secrecy, or is it simply the human tendency to perceive patterns where none exist?

Similar themes emerge when examining the assassinations of civil rights leaders. The murder of Martin Luther King Jr., for instance, not only shocked the nation but also sparked theories suggesting that government agencies may have played a role in suppressing dissent. The idea that a beloved figure advocating for equality could be silenced by those in power raises profound questions about the extent of state involvement in violence against its own citizens. The investigation into King's death remains shrouded in controversy, leaving many to wonder if the official narrative is merely a façade masking a darker truth.

The celebrity sphere isn't immune to the shadow of conspiracy either. The deaths of stars like Marilyn Monroe and John Lennon have spurred theories that suggest their assassinations were orchestrated by powerful interests wishing to silence them. Monroe's demise, often framed as a tragic overdose, has been linked to her connections with the Kennedy family, leading to speculation about motives that extend beyond personal conflicts. Similarly, Lennon's murder has prompted discussions about the implications of his anti-establishment views and whether he was seen as a threat to the status quo.

In the realm of modern conspiracy theories, the assassinations of key figures serve as a lens through which we can view broader societal fears about surveillance, control, and hidden agendas. The narratives surrounding these events often reflect deeper anxieties about the integrity of our institutions and the lengths to which those in power might go to protect their interests. As we peel back the layers of these historical tragedies, we find ourselves confronting not just the question of truth versus cover-up, but also the unsettling reality that the line between the two may be far more ambiguous than we are comfortable admitting.

The Deep State: Fact or Fiction?

The concept of the "Deep State" has surged into public
consciousness, captivating the minds of conspiracy theorists
and skeptics alike. This term typically refers to a clandestine
network of individuals within government and military circles
who allegedly operate independently of elected officials,
manipulating policy and decision-making from the shadows.
While some dismiss the idea as mere fiction, others assert that
there is a substantial reality behind it, rooted in historical
precedents and instances of government overreach. To truly
unravel this enigmatic phenomenon, one must delve into both
the documented instances that fuel these theories and the
psychological allure they hold.

Historically, the notion of a hidden power structure is not new. From the clandestine dealings of the Committee of 300 to the machinations of the Bilderberg Group, elite organizations have long been suspected of steering global events. These secretive gatherings often attract fervent speculation, as attendees include influential politicians, business moguls, and media tycoons. The veil of secrecy surrounding these meetings feeds the narrative that a select few hold the reins of power, far removed from public accountability. Such historical context lends credence to the idea that a "Deep State" might exist, silently orchestrating the fate of nations under the guise of democracy.

The modern political landscape has intensified the debate surrounding the Deep State, particularly in light of various scandals and whistleblower revelations. Instances like the Edward Snowden leaks and the revelations surrounding the CIA's covert operations have exposed the extent to which government agencies can operate without oversight. The implications of these findings sow distrust among citizens, leading many to believe that their elected representatives may not be the true decision-makers. This distrust is compounded by the frenetic pace of technological advancement, where surveillance capabilities expand at an alarming rate, further blurring the lines between transparency and secrecy in governance.

Critics of the Deep State theory often argue that it serves as a convenient scapegoat for political failures and societal frustrations. They contend that attributing complex governmental issues to a shadowy conspiracy detracts from the accountability of elected officials and the democratic process. This skepticism is valid; however, the fervency with which these theories persist suggests a deeper dissatisfaction with the status quo. As citizens grapple with perceived injustices and systemic corruption, the Deep State narrative offers a compelling, albeit unsettling, explanation for the chaos and disillusionment many feel in contemporary society.

Ultimately, whether one views the Deep State as fact or fiction may come down to individual interpretation of historical events and current realities. The interplay between truth and conspiracy is rarely black and white, particularly in an age where information is both abundant and obscured. The allure of the Deep State narrative lies not just in its potential veracity but also in its reflection of a collective yearning for transparency and integrity in governance. As we navigate the shadows of history, the exploration of such theories invites us to question the nature of power, the limits of oversight, and the very fabric of democracy itself.

Election Interference and Manipulation

In the labyrinth of historical events, the specter of election
interference and manipulation has loomed large, casting
shadows over democratic processes worldwide. From the
clandestine efforts of powerful elites to sway public opinion to
the more overt actions of foreign entities seeking to destabilize
nations, the narrative of election integrity is far more complex
than it appears. As we peel back the layers of this intricate
phenomenon, we uncover a tapestry woven with threads of
deception, ambition, and the relentless pursuit of power,
revealing just how deeply entrenched the manipulation of
elections is within the annals of history.

Consider the infamous case of the Watergate scandal, where political espionage unraveled the Nixon administration's grip on power, exposing a network of deceit that shook the very foundations of American democracy. The implications of such actions resonate beyond mere political machinations; they signify a broader pattern of governance where the ends justify the means. This episode serves as a reminder of how fragile democratic institutions can be and raises critical questions about accountability and transparency in the political arena. The echoes of Watergate reverberate through time, instilling a sense of skepticism that fuels contemporary conspiracy theories surrounding election integrity.

As we delve further, we encounter the chilling specter of foreign interference, a tactic that has become alarmingly prevalent in recent decades. The revelations surrounding Russia's involvement in the 2016 U.S. presidential election illustrate a new era of cyber warfare, where misinformation campaigns are waged in the shadows of social media platforms. The implications extend far beyond national borders; they highlight the vulnerability of democracies to external manipulation and the lengths to which some will go to influence the course of history. Such incidents raise eyebrows and ignite imaginations, leading to a proliferation of conspiracy theories that question the legitimacy of electoral outcomes and the motives behind them.

The intrigue doesn't stop at foreign players; domestic actors have also been implicated in the orchestration of electoral sabotage. From gerrymandering to voter suppression tactics, the manipulation of the electoral process reflects a deep-seated desire among some political factions to maintain power at any cost. These actions often incite outrage and fuel conspiracy theories that suggest a grander scheme at play, where secret societies and shadowy organizations pull the strings behind the scenes. These theories resonate with those who feel disenfranchised and suspicious of a system that seems rigged against them, further complicating the narrative of electoral integrity.

As we navigate this treacherous terrain, it becomes evident that the intersection of technology and surveillance has added a new layer of complexity to election interference. The rise of data analytics and targeted advertising has transformed how campaigns operate, often blurring the lines between ethical persuasion and manipulation. In an age where information can be weaponized, the potential for abuse is staggering. The conspiratorial lens through which many view these developments reflects a growing unease with the power dynamics at play, suggesting that the battle for electoral integrity is not merely a political struggle but a profound societal challenge that demands vigilance and scrutiny. The shadows of history remind us that the quest for truth in the face of manipulation is both a noble endeavor and an urgent necessity.

Chapter 10: Environmental Conspiracy Theories

Climate Change: A Hoax?

The notion that climate change is a hoax has gained traction among various groups, despite overwhelming scientific consensus on the issue. This perspective often hinges on the belief that climate change is exaggerated or fabricated for ulterior motives, such as political gain or economic profit. Proponents of this theory argue that a select few, often embedded within governmental or scientific institutions, manipulate data to instill fear and justify invasive policies. This skepticism feeds into a broader narrative of distrust towards authorities and experts, which is a hallmark of many conspiracy theories throughout history.

At the heart of the climate change denial movement is a complex interplay of historical events and societal beliefs. The industrial revolution marked a significant turning point, igniting a dependence on fossil fuels and elevating economic prosperity. As environmental concerns began to rise in the late 20th century, a counter-narrative emerged, suggesting that climate scientists were not just warning of impending doom but also exploiting the situation for financial gain through grants and funding. This narrative plays on deeply ingrained fears of losing economic stability and individual freedoms, further entrenching the belief that climate change is a manufactured crisis.

Celebrity culture has also played a role in shaping public perception of climate change. High-profile figures advocating for environmental action often find themselves at the center of conspiracy theories, accused of hypocrisy or using the climate agenda as a platform for personal gain. This sentiment resonates with those who view celebrity endorsements as insincere or driven by ulterior motives. The presence of influential personalities in the climate debate can thus complicate the dialogue, as their involvement may lead skeptics to dismiss the scientific consensus as mere celebrity-driven propaganda.

Moreover, the intertwining of climate change with political conspiracy theories cannot be overlooked. Some argue that climate policies are a means for governments to exert control over citizens, presenting environmental regulations as a guise for surveillance and restriction of personal liberties. This perspective taps into a rich vein of historical conspiracy theories where governmental authority is viewed with suspicion. The fear of an overreaching state, combined with the urgency of climate action, creates a fertile ground for narratives that frame environmentalism as a tool of oppression rather than an opportunity for societal improvement.

Ultimately, the debate over climate change as a hoax is emblematic of broader societal struggles regarding trust, authority, and the dissemination of information. As scientific evidence mounts and climate-related disasters become increasingly frequent, the challenge lies in bridging the gap between skepticism and acceptance. Understanding the historical context and motivations behind conspiracy theories can illuminate why some individuals cling to the idea of climate change as a hoax. By unraveling these layers, we can foster a more informed and constructive dialogue about one of the most pressing issues of our time.

Chemtrails: Debunked or Hidden Truth?

Chemtrails have emerged as one of the most provocative conspiracy theories of our time, captivating the imaginations of those who suspect that nefarious forces are at work in the skies above us. Proponents of this theory assert that the visible trails left by aircraft, commonly referred to as contrails, are not merely the result of condensation but rather a deliberate effort by governments or shadowy organizations to manipulate the climate, control the population, or even conduct experiments on unsuspecting citizens. This theory has sparked heated debates, with fervent believers claiming that these chemical trails are a form of geoengineering or population control, while skeptics dismiss it as a baseless myth. But what is the truth behind this contentious issue?

To unravel the mystery, it is crucial to understand the science behind contrails. When planes fly at high altitudes, the combination of hot engine exhaust and cold atmospheric conditions can lead to the formation of water vapor, which condenses and freezes into ice crystals, creating the white streaks we see in the sky. These contrails can persist for hours, depending on the humidity and temperature of the air. Scientific studies have consistently shown that these phenomena are a normal part of aviation and are entirely harmless. Nevertheless, the allure of a hidden agenda fuels the belief in chemtrails, as many are drawn to the idea that something as mundane as air travel could be part of a grand scheme.

The skepticism surrounding the official explanations has deep roots in historical mistrust of governments and institutions. The legacy of Cold War secrecy, coupled with revelations of past government experiments—such as MKUltra—has left many individuals questioning the transparency of their leaders. This context has allowed the chemtrail narrative to flourish, as it taps into a broader sentiment of paranoia and distrust. For those already inclined to believe in conspiracies, the idea that the government would engage in covert operations to control the population or alter the environment resonates deeply with their worldview.

Celebrity endorsements of the chemtrail theory further complicate the discourse. When influential figures voice their concerns about what they perceive as a dangerous practice, they lend credibility to the narrative, drawing in even more supporters. This phenomenon highlights the intersection of fame and conspiracy, where the platform of celebrity can amplify fringe ideas, potentially leading to a more extensive following. Yet, such endorsements often lack scientific grounding, relying instead on emotional appeals and anecdotal evidence, which can cloud rational judgment.

Ultimately, the debate over chemtrails serves as a microcosm of the larger conversation about truth in an age of information overload. With the rise of social media and alternative news sources, misinformation can spread rapidly, often outpacing factual rebuttals. As adults navigating this complex landscape, it is essential to approach such theories with a critical mindset, balancing curiosity with skepticism. While the allure of uncovering hidden truths is undeniably captivating, discerning fact from fiction is crucial in our quest for understanding the shadows of history and the conspiracies that haunt our collective imagination.

The Role of Corporations in Environmental Deception

The role of corporations in environmental deception is a fascinating yet troubling aspect of our modern narrative. As we peel back the layers of history, it becomes evident that many corporations have not only prioritized profits over the planet but have also actively engaged in misleading the public about their environmental impact. From oil giants to agribusiness, these entities have constructed elaborate facades, presenting a green image while simultaneously engaging in practices that wreak havoc on ecosystems. The manipulation of information, whether through subtle advertising or outright falsehoods, has created a web of deception that challenges our understanding of corporate responsibility and environmental stewardship.

One of the most striking examples of corporate environmental deception is the tobacco industry's historical denial of the health risks associated with smoking. This pattern of denial has echoes in the climate change debate, where fossil fuel companies have long funded research and campaigns that downplay the reality of global warming. By employing scientists and PR firms to create a smokescreen of doubt, they have influenced public perception and hindered legislative action. This strategy of sowing confusion is not unique to the fossil fuel sector; it has been replicated across various industries that have vested interests in maintaining the status quo, even as the planet faces unprecedented challenges.

Moreover, the phenomenon of "greenwashing" has emerged as a prominent tactic in corporate environmental deception. Companies often engage in marketing strategies that exaggerate their sustainability efforts while glossing over harmful practices. For instance, a corporation may tout its commitment to renewable energy while simultaneously investing billions in fossil fuel extraction. This deliberate misrepresentation not only deceives consumers but also undermines genuine efforts towards environmental conservation. As consumers become more environmentally conscious, the potential for corporations to exploit this awareness for profit grows, creating a complex landscape where authenticity is often overshadowed by marketing ploys.

The political implications of corporate environmental deception are equally significant. By wielding their financial power, corporations can influence policy decisions that prioritize their interests over the collective good. Lobbying efforts and campaign contributions create a symbiotic relationship between corporations and politicians, resulting in legislation that often favors corporate agendas at the expense of environmental protection. This intricate dance raises critical questions about the integrity of democratic processes and the extent to which corporate interests can shape public policy, further entrenching environmental degradation in the name of economic growth.

In the grand tapestry of conspiracy theories, the role of corporations in environmental deception stands as a stark reminder of the complexities we face as a society. As we grapple with the realities of climate change, pollution, and biodiversity loss, it is essential to remain vigilant against the narratives crafted by those who prioritize profit over planet. By uncovering the truth behind corporate practices and holding these entities accountable, we can illuminate the shadows of history and pave the way for a more sustainable future. The responsibility lies not only with the corporations but also with us, the informed citizens, to demand transparency and integrity in the environmental claims made by those who wield significant power over our planet.

Chapter 11: The Future of Conspiracy Theories

Evolving Narratives in a Digital Age

The digital age has revolutionized the way we consume information, reshaping the narratives that underpin historical events and contemporary issues. Gone are the days when a few authoritative voices dominated the conversation; today, a multitude of perspectives can be accessed with a single click. This democratization of information has given rise to a vibrant tapestry of conspiracy theories, allowing individuals to weave their own interpretations of events. From government cover-ups to celebrity scandals, the narratives surrounding these theories are evolving rapidly, influenced by the immediacy and accessibility of digital platforms.

Shadows of History: Unraveling the Great Conspiracy Theories of Our Time

Social media has become a breeding ground for the rapid dissemination of conspiracy theories, where ideas can spread like wildfire. The viral nature of content allows fringe theories to gain traction, sometimes overshadowing established facts. For instance, the rise of UFO and alien conspiracy theories has been fueled by online communities that share sightings and evidence, creating a collective narrative that often challenges mainstream scientific explanations. As these theories gain followers, they become part of a larger discourse that questions authority and the veracity of information provided by institutions, from governments to media outlets.

Moreover, the interplay between technology and conspiracy narratives is fascinating. Surveillance conspiracies, for example, have gained new life as advancements in technology introduce concerns about privacy and data security. The emergence of smart devices has led to suspicions about government monitoring and corporate espionage, prompting individuals to question the motives behind technological advancements. This skepticism permeates discussions surrounding financial and economic conspiracies, where the opacity of financial systems breeds distrust and fuels theories about manipulation and control by a select few. The narratives surrounding these conspiracies are not static; they change as new technologies emerge and as public awareness evolves.

Celebrity conspiracy theories have also adapted to the digital landscape, where public figures are scrutinized and dissected by fans and critics alike. From claims of hidden relationships to elaborate hoaxes, the celebrity culture thrives on speculation, often blurring the lines between fact and fiction. The immediacy of online platforms allows for real-time engagement with these narratives, enabling audiences to contribute to and shape the discourse. As a result, the evolving narratives around celebrity conspiracies reflect broader societal anxieties about fame, power, and the human desire for connection, even in the most fantastical scenarios.

Ultimately, the digital age has empowered individuals to become active participants in the creation and propagation of conspiracy theories. The narratives that emerge are not merely products of individual imagination; they are influenced by collective experiences, cultural contexts, and technological advancements. As we continue to navigate this landscape, it is crucial to remain vigilant and discerning, questioning not only the information we encounter but also the motivations behind it. In this ever-evolving digital tapestry, the shadows of history intertwine with the bright lights of modernity, creating a complex narrative that invites exploration and critical engagement.

The Impact of Social Media

The rise of social media has revolutionized the landscape of communication, enabling a rapid dissemination of information that has both illuminated and obscured the truths of our world. Within the realm of conspiracy theories, platforms like Twitter, Facebook, and Instagram have become breeding grounds for ideas that challenge mainstream narratives. The immediacy and reach of these platforms allow conspiracy theories to flourish and evolve at an unprecedented pace, often outpacing traditional media outlets. This dynamic environment fosters a unique ecosystem where ideas, no matter how outlandish, can gain traction and a loyal following almost overnight.

Social media has not only amplified the voices of conspiracy theorists but has also created a space where niche communities can thrive. Those interested in topics ranging from government cover-ups to UFO sightings can find like-minded individuals, facilitating discussions that might have been marginalized in conventional settings. This sense of community often reinforces beliefs, as members share personal anecdotes, curated content, and persuasive arguments that align with their views. The echo chamber effect can solidify convictions and make it increasingly challenging for individuals to consider alternative perspectives, further entrenching them in their chosen narratives.

Moreover, the algorithms driving social media platforms prioritize engagement over accuracy, often promoting sensational content that captures attention. This can lead to a distortion of reality, where conspiracy theories are presented with the same visibility as factual reporting. The result is a world where misinformation can spread like wildfire, leading to a populace that is often more inclined to believe in sensational claims than nuanced truths. This phenomenon has serious implications for how society consumes information, as the line between fact and fiction becomes increasingly blurred, particularly in the context of political and environmental issues.

The impact of social media on the perception of celebrities has also been profound. Conspiracy theories surrounding public figures often gain traction when their lives are scrutinized through the lens of social media. Rumors of secret societies, hidden agendas, and elaborate cover-ups can spread rapidly, fueled by the viral nature of posts and shares. This not only affects the reputations of those involved but also reflects a broader cultural fascination with the idea that powerful individuals operate behind the scenes, manipulating events for their own gain. The allure of insider knowledge keeps audiences engaged, as they sift through layers of speculation and conjecture to uncover the 'truth.'

As we navigate this digital age, the impact of social media on conspiracy theories remains a double-edged sword. On one hand, it democratizes information and gives a voice to the marginalized; on the other, it fosters an environment ripe for misinformation and divisive rhetoric. Understanding this complex relationship is vital for unraveling the intricate web of conspiracy theories that permeate our society today. As we delve deeper into the shadows of history, we must remain vigilant, discerning the truths from the fabrications that thrive in the age of social media.

How to Navigate the Sea of Misinformation

In an age where information flows faster than ever, navigating the sea of misinformation can feel like a daunting task. The digital landscape is awash with theories and claims that can easily distort the truth. Whether you're delving into the murky waters of government cover-ups, celebrity scandals, or the enigmatic world of UFOs, it's crucial to arm yourself with the tools that will help you sift through the noise and uncover the facts. Start by fostering a healthy skepticism; question everything, but do so with a balanced mind. This means being open to new ideas while critically evaluating their credibility before accepting them as truth.

Shadows of History: Unraveling the Great Conspiracy Theories of Our Time

One of the most effective strategies for navigating misinformation is to hone your research skills. Dive deep into reputable sources that offer well-researched and fact-checked information. Academic journals, established news outlets, and expert analyses provide a solid foundation for understanding complex topics. When exploring conspiracy theories, it's essential to distinguish between sensationalized narratives and those grounded in verified evidence. Utilize fact-checking websites to verify claims that seem extraordinary; these resources can be invaluable in uncovering the truth behind the headlines and social media posts.

Engaging with a diverse range of perspectives can also illuminate the shadows of history. Conspiracy theories often thrive in echo chambers, where similar viewpoints are reinforced without challenge. By actively seeking out opposing perspectives, you can enrich your understanding of the topic at hand. This doesn't mean you have to agree with every viewpoint; rather, it encourages critical thinking and helps to identify biases in both your own beliefs and those of others. The more angles you explore, the clearer the picture becomes, allowing you to navigate through the fog of misinformation with greater clarity.

Community discussion plays a vital role in unraveling conspiracy theories as well. Joining forums, attending lectures, or participating in book clubs focused on historical conspiracies can provide you with a wealth of knowledge and fresh insights. Engaging with others who are equally passionate about uncovering the truth can foster a sense of camaraderie while sharpening your analytical skills. Sharing thoughts and debating ideas in a constructive environment can lead to new revelations and a deeper understanding of the often intricate web of conspiracies that permeate our history.

Finally, remain vigilant and adaptable. The landscape of misinformation is constantly evolving, with new theories emerging and old ones being debunked. Staying informed about current events and ongoing research in relevant fields will aid you in recognizing when a conspiracy theory may be gaining traction unjustly. By committing to lifelong learning and maintaining a curious mindset, you not only empower yourself to navigate the complexities of misinformation but also contribute to a more informed society. Embracing this journey will allow you to face the shadows of history with confidence and discernment, ultimately revealing the truths that lie hidden beneath the surface.

About the Author

This author goes by the name SEA62 books Aho. She resides in a quaint
town in southern Ontario, Canada. She lives with her husband and
their dog, Maggie. Their three children having since left the nest. They enjoy a
quiet life with retirement looming on the horizon. In the meantime they enjoy
household chores, nature walks, gardening, swimming, quilting, and of course
reading.

Living in Southern Ontario gives a unique perspective of all things in the US.
Especially the past 10 years or so. Listening to the unbelievable Consipiracy
Theories and being aware of the global effect of such theories as: Roswell The
crash that shook the world to Is Elvis still alive?, secret government, financial,
global warming. and societal norms. Whew what a lot of ....
Anyway a compilation of the theories hopefully puts to rest some of the angles
worked into everyday life and this author enjoyed the research into such
conspiracies. There is plenty to keep you entertained!
Enjoy!

Made in United States
Troutdale, OR
12/14/2024

26515213R00084